A SONG FOR THE HORSE NATION

Horses in Native American Cultures

Edited by George P. Horse Capture and
Emil Her Many Horses

With additional essays by Herman J. Viola and Linda R. Martin

National Museum of the American Indian, Smithsonian Institution
Washington, D.C., and New York, in association with
Fulcrum Publishing, Golden, Colorado

Text Credits

Captions by George P. Horse Capture (A'aninin) and Emil Her Many Horses (Oglala Lakota)

"Horse Society" and accompanying songs as well as "Old Buffalo's War Narrative" from *Teton Sioux Music* by Frances Densmore (Washington: Smithsonian Institution Bureau of American Ethnology, 1918).

"A Warrior to His Horse" from *Sioux and Chippewa Songs* by Frances Densmore, published privately in Washington, D.C., 1917. Reprinted in *Frances Densmore and American Indian Music: A Memorial Volume*, edited by Charles Hofmann (New York: Museum of the American Indian/Heye Foundation, 1968).

"I Would Steal Horses" from *First Indian on the Moon* by Sherman Alexie (New York: Hanging Loose Press, 1993). Reprinted by permission of the publisher.

"Blue Horses Rush In" from *Sáanii Dahataał: The Women Are Singing* by Luci Tapahonso (Tucson: University of Arizona Press, 1993). Reprinted by permission of the publisher.

Photo Credits

The photographers, when known, of images from the Photo Archives of the National Museum of the American Indian are identified in the captions that accompany each photo. The photographers of the objects from the NMAI's collection are listed below.

Pamela Dewey: 6, 86
Katherine Fogden (Akwesasne Mohawk): 13,18, 21, 24, 25–29, 32–35, 37–40, 47–49, 51, 53, 54–60, 69, 80, 82–85, 88
Karen Furth: 20, 68, 72
Carmelo Guadagno: 4, 22–23
David Heald: 19, 52, 65, 67, 70, 71, 73, 74, 76, 77, 81, 87
Janine Sarna Jones: 50, 75, 89

Cover image: Assiniboine horse stick. Made by Medicine Bear, circa 1860. Photograph by Katherine Fogden. 11/8044

Back cover image: Chaticksi (Pawnee) child on horseback. P14190

Inside cover image, front and back: Driving in the saddle horses. Wyoming. Photograph by the L. M. H. Company. P14524

Frontispiece: Absaroke (Crow) chiefs, from left: Holds the Enemy, Plenty Coups, and two who are unidentified, early 20th century. Montana. Photograph by Willem Wildschut. N31111

Publications Manager: Tanya Thrasher
Editors: Amy Pickworth and Sally Barrows

The National Museum of the American Indian, Smithsonian Institution, is committed to advancing knowledge and understanding of the Native cultures of the Western Hemisphere, past, present, and future, through partnership with Native people and others. The museum works to support the continuance of culture, traditional values, and transitions in contemporary Native life. The museum's publishing program seeks to augment awareness of Native American beliefs and lifeways and to educate the public about the history and significance of Native cultures.
www.AmericanIndian.si.edu

Library of Congress Cataloging-in-Publication Data
A song for the horse nation: horses in Native American cultures / National Museum of the American Indian.
     p. cm.
   Edited by George P. Horse Capture and Emil Her Many Horses.
   ISBN 1-55591-112-9 (pbk.)
   1. Horses–North America–History. 2. Indians of North America–Domestic animals. 3. Indians of North America–Hunting. 4. Indians of North America–War. 5. Human-animal relationships–North America–History. I. Emil Her Many Horses. II. George P. Capture. III. National Museum of the American Indian (U.S.) IV. Title.

E98.H55S66 2006
636.100973–dc22

                                    2005030109

ISBN: 978-1-55591-112-6

Printed in China
0 9 8 7 6 5 4

Design: Amy Thornton, Ann Douden

Fulcrum Publishing
4690 Table Mountain Drive, Suite 100
Golden, Colorado 80403
800-992-2908 • 303-277-1623
www.fulcrumbooks.com

Table of Contents

Foreword   *Kevin Gover* 5

Introduction: Freedom, Bravery, and Generosity:
  Native Americans and the Horse   *Herman J. Viola* 7

Remembering Lakota Ways   *Emil Her Many Horses* 11

Typecast Indians   *Linda R. Martin*. 14

Horse Trappings and Ornament. 18

Horse Equipment   *George P. Horse Capture* 36

Horse Society   *Frances Densmore* 41

Horse Images in Everyday Life 47

The Art of Capturing Horses:
  Joe Medicine Crow Counts Coup during World War II
  Herman J. Viola 61

Old Buffalo's War Narrative   *as told to Frances Densmore* 63

"I Would Steal Horses"   *Sherman Alexie*. 68

"Affinity: Mustang"   *Linda Hogan* 91

"Blue Horses Rush In"   *Luci Tapahonso* 93

Man Who Carries the Sword *(Oglala Lakota), circa 1875. 10/9628*

Records show that this artist is Lakota, but some details suggest that the subject may be from a southern Plains tribe.

The horseman wears an impressive bonnet with many feathers and carries a shield with feathers as well, indicating that he was a very prominent warrior. His horse wears a beautiful silver bridle, and the single horn on the warrior's headdress is likely a personal reference, possibly from a dream.

In today's world, red feathers are given as a sign of respect to Native veterans who have been wounded in battle, and a number of contemporary Indian ceremonies—including the honoring songs sung at powwows—pay tribute to veterans.

"Man-who-carries-the-Sword"

Foreword

HORSE NATION

If we are to understand the significance of horses for many North American Indians—especially those tribes of the Great Plains—a series of stories must be told. One of these narratives has to do with the transformation of Native cultures following the arrival of the horse in the eighteenth century. With horses came great change—the near-simultaneous introduction of horses and guns radically altered both Plains warfare and Native economies. Horses created new tribal tensions and caused old ones to flare, encouraging entirely new strategies on and off the battlefield between tribes and against waves of settlers. The combination of horses and guns transformed the dynamic of the hunt as well, allowing buffalo and other animals important to trade to be tracked farther and dispatched more easily. As beasts of burden, horses literally lightened the load of everyday life, ushering in a cultural efflorescence on the Plains. As coeditor George P. Horse Capture succinctly puts it, "Because of the horse, tribes had something they had never had before: unencumbered time to develop their arts, spirituality, and philosophy."

Here we turn to another kind of story: the horse as a subject central to Indian expressive culture, whether in the form of objects or words or music. A beloved companion admired for its keen intellect and remarkable beauty, the horse has been portrayed in paint, beads, and quills on shirts, hide robes, and dresses. And our horses themselves have been outfitted in stunning accoutrements. There is an abiding affinity here; the name of this book is in fact taken from a Teton Lakota song recorded at the turn of the twentieth century by scholar Frances Densmore:

> out of the earth
> I sing for them
> A Horse nation
> I sing for them…

This is one of many odes and elegies praising the bravery and devotion of horses, who continue to be evoked as powerful symbols in contemporary poems by Sherman Alexie, Luci Tapahonso, and Linda Hogan.

This book was first published in 2006, and I'm pleased that the work begun here continued after the first printing. In 2009, we opened an exhibition, also titled *A Song for the Horse Nation*, that featured these and other objects from our collections, along with expanded historical and cultural commentary. The exhibition, which debuted at our George Gustav Heye Center in New York and traveled to our museum on the National Mall, is also accompanied by a website, www.nmai.si.edu/exhibitions/horsenation, which will exist long after the show ends.

As historian Herman Viola writes in his excellent introduction, "America's Native peoples have little for which to thank Christopher Columbus except the horse." Columbus aside, there are several people I wish to thank for their work on *A Song for the Horse Nation*. Curator

Emil Her Many Horses (Oglala Lakota) has been critical to every phase of this project, from the book's manuscript to new research for the exhibition to the launch of the website. Former head of publications Terence Winch originally conceived of this book and was the first to suggest an exhibition. And the participation of George P. Horse Capture (A'aninin), Senior Counselor to the Director Emeritus, was invaluable. I would like to extend a special thanks to George for his role in the development of this book and so many other projects during his tenure with the museum. Finally, I suppose we might thank the horses themselves, who conjure much of the best we remember and aspire to.

Detail from pictographic drawing on page 86. Artist unknown (Hidatsa), Exploits of Poor Wolf, Hidatsa Second Chief, *probably early 20th century. 4/2446A*

—**Kevin Gover**

(Pawnee)

Director, National Museum of the American Indian

Introduction

FREEDOM, BRAVERY, AND GENEROSITY
NATIVE AMERICANS AND THE HORSE

The image of warriors wearing eagle feather war bonnets and galloping across prairie grasses astride painted ponies is so ingrained in our psyche that it is hard to imagine a time when horses were not a part of the American landscape. If pressed on the subject, some people would probably say that Indians on horseback welcomed the settlers at Jamestown or the Pilgrims at Plymouth Rock. Even well-read Americans, however, would probably be startled to learn that the Indian horse culture of the Great Plains was a rather brief moment in the history of North America, little more than a hundred years. In truth, horses reached the Great Plains at about the time of the French and Indian War, and that romantic, buffalo-hunting, horse-dependent culture of the Plains Indians was virtually gone—with the buffalo—when the United States celebrated its centennial in 1876. But while it lasted, the marriage of horse and Indian was a joy to behold and a thing of beauty, as these treasures from the NMAI so well express.

America's Native peoples have little for which to thank Christopher Columbus except the horse. Although the horse had originated in the Americas more than forty million years ago, it had become extinct in its homeland after spreading to other parts of the world, and it was Columbus who returned horses to the Western Hemisphere after an absence of some ten thousand years. His cargo on his second voyage in 1493 included twenty-five horses of Andalusian ancestry.

At first, the horses scared the Indians. They had never seen an animal that could carry a person. They called the horses "sky dogs," believing that they were monsters or messengers from the heavens. The first Hopi to see horses paved their way with ceremonial blankets.

Awe quickly gave way to a desire to obtain these wonderful creatures, but the Spanish were equally desirous of keeping them out of Indian hands, knowing that horses would give Native Americans a powerful tool for protecting their land from invasion. Nonetheless, by the late 1700s, virtually every tribe in the Far West was mounted or at least had access to horses (some of the mountain tribes ate rather than rode theirs). How did this happen?

Historians once credited Francisco Coronado and Hernando de Soto for this remarkable accomplishment, claiming their runaways were responsible for the vast herds of mustangs that eventually roamed the West, but subsequent research has discredited this theory. Although both expeditions were well mounted—Coronado, for instance, had 558 horses—their horses could not have contributed to the wild horse herds because of the simple fact that Spanish law required soldiers to ride stallions. Thus, of Coronado's 558 horses, only two were mares, and both were returned to New Spain. The generally accepted explanation now is that the Indians acquired their horses from Spanish herds in New Mexico. Some they captured, but the bulk they obtained as a result of the Pueblo Uprising of 1680.

As New Spain expanded, the Spanish eventually moved into what is now the United States, establishing a large colony in Santa Fe, the heartland of the Pueblo Indians. For the better part of a century, these placid people endured Spanish ecclesiastical and political domination before rising in rebellion under Pope, a Tewa religious leader from San Juan Pueblo. Their sole purpose in rebelling was to expel the Spanish from their country, which they accomplished with remarkable ease.

Detail from Taos Pueblo buffalo hide robe on page 56. 5/719

Pope assaulted Santa Fe, killing some five hundred Spaniards and forcing a thousand more to flee southward. Left behind were sheep, goats, cattle, and hundreds of horses, which the Pueblo people traded to neighboring tribes. From New Spain, the horse population expanded rapidly across North America, moving north and east along established trading networks that existed between the various Indian tribes.

The value of horses was so readily apparent that most tribes, on learning of the new and marvelous creatures, wasted little time in acquiring some. Indeed, imagine confronting an enemy on a horse for the first time. One such witness was a Cree Indian named Saukamaupee, who told his story to Hudson's Bay fur trader David Thompson during the winter of 1787–88. As a young man, Saukamaupee had lived with the Piegan Indians, who are Canadian relatives of the Blackfeet. The Piegan were continually at war with their Shoshone neighbors, and

Saukamaupee participated in several fights. In his first one, which took place in about 1730, several Shoshones were riding horses, a creature he and his Piegan friends had never before seen. Swinging their stone war clubs, the mounted Shoshones charged and quickly routed the Piegans.

Soon after, the Piegan got their first close look at a Shoshone horse, which had died from an arrow wound in its belly. "Numbers of us went to see him," Saukamaupee recalled, "and we all admired him. He put us in mind of a stag that had lost his horns, and we did not know what name to give him. But as he was a slave to man, like the dog, which carried our things, he was named the Big Dog." Later, because horses were the size of elks, the Piegan began calling them *ponokomita*, or "elk dog," which is still their word for horse.

The horse drew some tribes onto the Great Plains. The gun chased others out of the eastern woodlands. At the same time that horses were moving north from Mexico, guns were moving

Driving in the saddle horses. Wyoming. Photograph by the L. M. H. Company. P14524

west from New England. The English, the Dutch, and the French began trading and selling guns to Indians even though everyone knew that Indians with guns would become a formidable foe in battle. As the eastern tribes got guns, they began to make war on their neighbors to the west. Eventually, tribes such as the Sioux, the Cheyenne, and Crow, who lived in the area of the Great Lakes, were forced to move onto the Great Plains. There they got horses coming from the other direction. In time, they also got guns from the east. The result was the mounted Plains warrior, who became a feared opponent as the United States fulfilled its Manifest Destiny.

Horses became an integral part of the culture of many western tribes, such as the Nez Perce and Blackfeet of the far Northwest, the Kiowa and Comanche of the southern Plains, and the Arapaho, Crow, Cheyenne, and Sioux of the northern Plains. Young men would risk life and limb to enter the villages of enemy tribes in order to capture a prized horse staked near its owner's tipi. Capturing an enemy's horse was a coup, a great achievement meriting praise and honor from family and friends. Plains oral histories abound with stories of lucky and luckless young men who made horse capturing an art. After returning from a successful raid astride a fine horse, a proud young man more often than not would give his prize to a widow or other unfortunate member of the community, thereby manifesting his generosity as well as his bravery.

The horse culture of the Plains Indians ended in the 1870s. A combination of factors caused its demise, but essentially, there were too many white people and too few buffalo. Where once the Plains Indians had roamed at will across the endless prairies of the West, they were now rooted on barren patches of soil and forced to learn a new lifestyle they neither wanted nor understood. Adding insult to injury, the federal government also dismounted these splendid riders in the attempt to make them yeoman farmers. But try as it might, the government could never fully erase their love of horses, and to this day, many of these tribes still consider horses a fundamental part of their culture. To them, horses will always symbolize freedom, bravery, and generosity. Indeed, as in days past, when a young man would give away a horse he had captured at the risk of his life, many Indians still give them away to friends and loved ones. Frequently, this is done in a powwow ceremony known as "the giveaway." Powwows are tribal gatherings much like family parties, where friends and relatives meet once a year to renew old friendships, dance, and carry on the traditions of their past.

This is especially evident at the Crow Fair, the grand powwow held annually on the Crow Reservation in southeastern Montana. One night at the 1991 fair, Crow families gave away six horses. These are a people who today drive pickup trucks or cars, for whom horses are no longer needed for transportation. Because of this, I asked a Crow friend if horses were really still important to Crow people. My question shocked him. "Herman," he said, "a Crow man would no more want to be seen riding a sorry-looking horse than he would want to have disobedient children. And a good friend, a good clan uncle, a good son-in-law deserves a good horse. Last year, my three daughters came to the house for Christmas dinner, and I told their husbands to look under the Christmas tree, where there was an empty bridle for each of them. 'In the spring,' I told them, 'go to my pasture and pick out the horse you want from my herd. It is my gift to you for being such good husbands to my daughters.'"

—Herman J. Viola
Curator Emeritus, National Museum of Natural History, Smithsonian Institution

Remembering Lakota Ways

My last name, Her Many Horses, is the Lakota name of my paternal great-grandmother. A more accurate English translation of her name is Many Horses Woman, meaning that she owned many horses. Among Lakota people, horses were a means of measuring wealth, but a far more important demonstration of wealth was the gesture of *giving away* horses in honor of a family member. Generosity is more important than possession.

"The Fourth of July used to be a good time," Grace Pourier, my maternal grandmother, recalled. I liked to listen to her stories about what Lakota life was like in the early 1900s. She knew her Lakota ways as they had been passed on to her by her relatives. Born in 1907 on Pine Ridge Reservation and raised on Horse Head Ranch in Manderson, South Dakota, she remembered how community members and extended family gathered to celebrate with giveaways, traditional dances, parades, and feasts. Later in life, she said she wished her grandmother had made her pay more attention to the events surrounding her, but at the time, she was just a kid having fun.

Much of traditional Lakota culture was threatened in the early 1900s. After the Lakota people were placed on reservations in the late 1800s, the U.S. government forbade their language and ceremonial life. Lakota people continued their traditions by incorporating traditional dances and giveaways into the Independence Day (and other American holiday) festivities in which they were encouraged to participate. For this reason, Fourth of July celebrations became something to look forward to. After Lakota men joined the military to fight in World War I, the use of the U.S. flag in beadwork and quillwork took on a new meaning. Today, if a bead worker uses the flag design, he or she is probably a veteran or a family member of someone who has served in the military.

In the early years of my grandmother's youth, horses still played an important role in the lives of the Oglala Lakota people. Since their introduction to the region in the early 1700s, horses had revolutionized Plains cultures. But they were more than work animals; horses were, and still are, cherished. The Pourier family was known for its racehorses. During the reservation period of the early 1900s, beautiful beaded horse head covers, saddle blankets, and saddlebags were made to decorate favorite horses on special occasions, such as the Fourth of July parades. Horses were often given away at naming ceremonies, memorial ceremonies (held a year after a family member's death), and giveaways (which might celebrate a returning veteran or honor a graduating student). Traditional giveaways centered on the giving away of horses, money, clothing, blankets, and other material objects. Hosting a giveaway today involves tremendous preparation, including the gathering of gifts, such as brightly colored star quilts, Pendleton blankets, and handmade shawls, as well as feeding the whole community.

Grandma Grace once told me that her grandmother really knew Indian ways: "Grandpa Pourier would have been a rich man, but Grandma Pourier kept giving the horses away." A horse to be given away would be brought into the Fourth of July dance arbor or other community gathering, while men on horseback waited outside. The horse was shown to the people or paraded inside the arbor, then taken outside, given a slap on the rump, and released. The man on horseback fortunate enough to catch the freed horse became its proud new owner.

Phillip Whiteman, Jr., at the Denver March Powwow, 2001, giving away one of his horses. Photograph by Emil Her Many Horses

My grandmother also remembered that women would give away dresses made of tanned deer hide, with the yoke of the dress completely covered with beadwork. "They would take off their beaded dresses right there in the dance arbor and give them away." The woman giving the dress away wore a cloth dress beneath the beaded dress. Giving away a fully beaded dress in honor of a relative was a tremendous act of generosity. The person receiving the valuable gift would shake hands with the giver and with the relative being honored.

Emily Her Many Horses, my paternal grandmother, remembered receiving her Lakota name at about age ten. She wore a wool dress embellished with many elk teeth, valuable because only two of each elk's teeth—the incisors—are used for decoration. They are natural ivory. Along with this dress, she wore beaded moccasins and leggings, and after the naming ceremony, she was told to give away the dress, moccasins, and leggings. She struggled to keep the dress, but her parents made her part with it—at such a young age, she did not understand what this act of generosity meant, and she wondered why her grandfather had her shoes, which were tied together by their shoestrings and thrown over his saddle horn. Her grandfather gave away five horses that day in her honor.

Leo Her Many Horses, my father, was given a horse at a Hunka Lowanpi, a naming ceremony held during a Sun Dance. He received a wooden stick that had attached to it a rawhide cutout of a horse. This meant that he would later receive the actual horse. The Hunka Lowanpi is a Lakota naming/adoption ceremony. It creates a kinship relationship that is respected by all the family members involved, and it is at this ceremony that Lakota names are given. The family of the person receiving the name will ask a well-respected individual to name its relative. The person naming the individual will pray with an eagle feather and then tie the feather in that person's hair. The names given at a Hunka Lowanpi are used only on special occasions—to have one's name sung publicly in a song is considered a great honor. The person whose name was sung or his or her family members will give away money, horses, or blankets for this honor.

Often on Memorial Day or after a death, people will place articles of clothing, bowls of fruit, packs of cigarettes, or other such items on the grave of a family member. These things are put out with the idea that other people are welcome to come by and take them. This act is performed to honor the deceased family member. My father said that one method of giving a horse away was to place the horse outside the cemetery with the reins left hanging loose to signify that anyone was welcome to take it.

In the collection of the National Museum of the American Indian, there is a beautiful, elaborately beaded horse head cover used at a 1904 Fourth of July parade at Pine Ridge, where my grandmother would be born three years later. The catalog information states that this horse head cover was collected by J. W. Good and was "used by chief of Teton Sioux to lead parade." Imagine the horse that wore this, the white beads glinting in the July sun.

It's a wonderful piece of artistry in its geometric design and lazy-stitch technique, but what's unique about it is that it appears to have been made with the intention of later being recycled into many different objects. The beaded section, which would be placed over the face of the horse, could be remade into a pair of women's beaded leggings, and the area over the horse's cheek could be made into a pipe bag. The upper neck section of the cover would have been made into a pair of tipi bags, also known as a "possible bag," because anything possible was stored inside. The lower neck section could be made into a pair of moccasins.

The resourceful woman who created this horse mask obviously had future plans for it—plans that were, fortunately for us, never carried out. A fusion of gifts never given, it is a reminder of Lakota traditions pieced together, a silent testament to what lies hidden within all those Fourths of July.

—Emil Her Many Horses (Oglala Lakota)

Lakota beaded horse mask, circa 1904. Pine Ridge Reservation, South Dakota. 1413

Typecast Indians

As a child in the early 1970s, I conceived many notions about family, identity, and life roles by sitting in front of my grandmother's television set. Raised in the city by my non-Native mother and grandmother, I learned about single-parenting issues from *A Family Affair* and *The Courtship of Eddie's Father*. My female role models, Mary Tyler Moore and Rhoda, were stylish, independent, career-minded women, much like my mother. My first impression of Native culture also came by way of television, through the genre of Hollywood Westerns. On celluloid, garishly painted, red-faced actors portrayed Natives as savage scalpers and merciless killers bent on unspeakable acts of murder and violation.

In films such as *War Arrow* (1953), wild "Kioways" on the warpath madly circle wagon trains of doomed pioneers. In *Kit Carson* (1940), other pioneers in peril are saved from Shoshone attacks as they ramble through Monument Valley, Utah. In the end, the hero—a frontier scout, cavalryman, or cowboy—gets the girl, and the Indian meets a grisly death. These death scenes, humorous and horrendous, involved dramatic feats of demoralizing comeuppance: an Indian brave shot from his war pony, somersaulting into the sagebrush, or shot and dragged behind his pony, arms flailing pitifully. Unfortunately, many other children my age drew the same conclusion about Indians as I did: we were dirty savages and merciless killers of women and children. Being the only Native American in my grade school, I became the target of hollering, war whoops, and hand-to-mouth "Indian" chanting.

Colored postcard showing Blackfeet man and woman on horseback. Glacier National Park, Montana. P16749

Through illustration, portraiture, photography, journalism, and film, generations of Native people have been haunted by the cultural stereotypes of the past five centuries. Seventeenth-century European illustrations of Iroquois scalpers, battle reenactments in Buffalo Bill's Wild West shows, dime novels, and souvenir postcards, for instance, have shaped the public's erroneous sentiments about Native Americans. Depending on the political agenda of the time—

whether in Europe or North America—the evolution of Native identity in the popular press has been dominated by two extreme stereotypes: savage marauder or docile member of a conquered race.

Colored lithograph of men in traditional dress on horseback. P14480

This may be from a Wild West show or similar endeavor.

In the United States, portraying Native Americans in a hostile light justified extreme measures in Indian policy, such as the use of brutal military force, land theft, and treaty violations. The idea of Indians as uncivilized and un-Christian also legit-imized forced conversions, mandatory attendance at boarding schools, and other religious abuses.

A century ago, the popular pastime of postcard collecting created a market for a flood of images that greatly contributed to the miseducation of several generations of Americans about who Indians are. To me, the seemingly benign photographs document the success of the lengthy and exhaustive U.S. military campaign to forcibly obtain Indian lands. By the late nineteenth century, most tribes had been relegated to reservations, creating dependence on government subsidies. Other forms of dependence and need manifested themselves in the extremes of religion or alcoholism. No matter the grim reality, in the postcard images, Indians and horses are paired to create a sense of nostalgia and security—a commercial device to lure homesteaders and financiers to the newly tamed West.

Colored postcard of Cree man in traditional dress on horseback. P16618

It appears that the warrior pictured here has been cut out and given another back-ground, a technique common to images in this genre.

Westward expansion gave rise to the railway, tourism, and mass production. Adventure-seeking travelers were lured west by the brochures and souvenir books produced by companies such as the Santa Fe Railroad and the Fred Harvey Company, whose advertising images promised the thrill of Indian encounters.

Unfortunately, the posed portraits in both postcards and brochures created misconceptions and false expectations about American Indians. Images like these continue to serve as a kitschy measuring stick of "Indian-ness," warping our own sense of Native identity and expression even as we modernize our communities and strive to continue our traditions in language, ceremonies, and arts.

These types of images have led to the commercial manufacture and gaudy interpretation of the most sacred Native objects. Curios come in a variety of forms, from hideous war bonnets

Pawnee Bill Wild West Show, circa 1928.
Pawnee, Oklahoma. Photograph by
Horace Poolaw (Kiowa). P26505

John C. Martin (Navajo) on Skipper, who
is part quarter horse and part Appaloosa,
on family land near Chaco Canyon, New
Mexico. Photograph courtesy of Linda R.
Martin.

and grotesque collector dolls to the "End of the Trail" belt buckles found in airport gift shops. In turn, these representations—usually in the visage of iconic chiefs and alluring Native maidens—reach large-scale international audiences through the mediums of Hollywood productions and sports team logos as well as vehicle, clothing, and food brands. To add insult to injury, the mass-produced appropriations create untold prosperity for everyone but the tribes themselves.

From century-old postcards to contemporary logos, these stereotypical images have distorted and oversimplified our cultures. They have created false understandings of the traditions of the hundreds of tribes that have their own languages, stories, art forms, and ceremonies. The self-esteem of our youth is damaged as they recoil from these grotesqueries and eventually their own true cultures. Ironically, our communities have often become dependent on perpetuating these Hollywood ideals in order to sustain any measure of economic stability.

Yet, as we endeavor to share with the world our unique voices and lifeways, our communities are increasingly empowered to redefine and celebrate our authentic identities. At the heart of my own nostalgic quest for the Indian and his horse, I need not look any further than my own photo albums. Today, one of my most cherished photographs is of my dad, John C. Martin, and his horse Skipper.

Photographed on family land near Chaco Canyon, New Mexico, he is the image of a real Indian, a hardworking, spiritual man who has embodied many different identities throughout his life: husband, father, grandfather, educator, tribal councilman, businessman, and rancher. But he's truly a Navajo cowboy at heart.

—Linda R. Martin (Navajo)

"A social chat after a sham Assiniboine raid," circa 1906. Montana. Photograph by Sumner Matteson. P21437

Photographer Sumner Matteson (1867–1920) documented many Assiniboine activities over a period of several years. This photo shows a sham battle between the Assiniboine and A'aninin, two tribes that traditionally had been enemies and that were, ironically, moved to the same reservation.

To relive the old days, sham battles were staged between opposing tribes. The groups would dress in their finery and meet up to wrestle, unhorse each other, and participate in hand-to-hand confrontations. Although no one was killed in these events, they were competitive and intense. After the victors were declared, everyone would celebrate with a feed.

Horse Trappings and Ornament

The most basic struggle of any people is to survive, a goal that is often limited by what is available. In the early buffalo days, life was difficult for American Indians, primarily because they were limited to walking and could only travel so far every day. Most of their waking hours were spent procuring sustenance, and there was little time for anything else. Hunting involved days of planning, with many in the community taking part. Securing food was all-important.

When horses arrived, these restrictions were loosened considerably. A lone hunter could obtain a buffalo almost at will, and tribes could travel farther, expanding their access to natural resources. Because of the horse, tribes had something they had never had before: unencumbered time to develop their arts, spirituality, and philosophy.

Most tribes embraced this new "big dog," and it fit easily within their cultures. The impact of this wonderful animal can be seen and felt in many creative and meaningful ways. The Menominee people of Wisconsin are said to have created this saddle, although other tribes used similar motifs. Brass tacks accent the curve of the neck. Can you imagine riding a horse upon a horse?

Northern Cheyenne quilled horse mask, mid-19th century. 1/4443

All peoples love aesthetics, and Plains tribes decorated their horses from bridle to tail. Because they limited a horse's range of vision, masks were usually used only for parades, not for battles.

This is a wonderful example of a quilled horse head covering. A piece such as this would have been created by a member of a quillwork guild. If a Cheyenne woman wanted to learn quill-work, she made an offering to a member of the guild, and if her offering was accepted, she would be taught the art and allowed to work as an apprentice. Not only were the quillwork guilds instructional, but they embodied a religious element as well, not unlike a sisterhood. To become a member of a quillwork guild was to assume a station of respect and power, and when the guilds died out in the late 1800s, so did the practice of quillwork in Cheyenne society.

Siksika (Blackfoot) horse head covering,
circa 1845. 18/8880

Picture a horse wearing this mask and
running toward you, and it isn't hard to
appreciate how powerful and utterly
transformative this head covering would
be. Possessing strong spiritual overtones,
this piece is decorated with pony beads,
clipped feathers, and Chinese brass
buttons.

Sarsi pad saddle, circa 1880. 1/1114

Saddles such as this one, appropriate both for show and for daily use, allowed warriors maximum mobility on the battlefield.

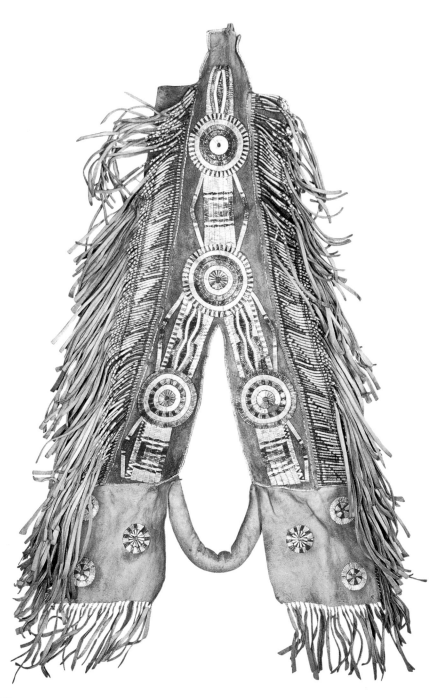

Cree or Red River Métis horse crupper,
circa 1850. Manitoba, Canada. 18/5498

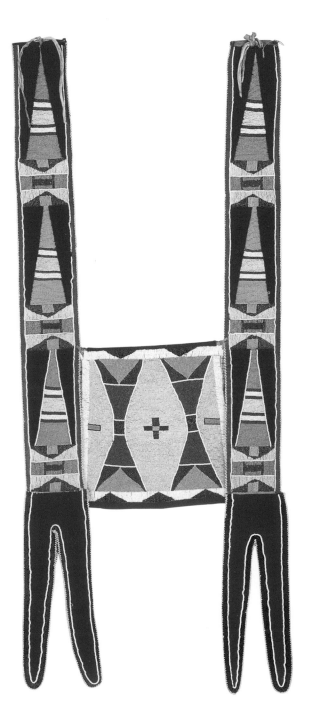

Absaroke (Crow) horse ornament, circa 1890. 20/7717

This beautiful beaded piece was made to hang across a horse's chest, but, unlike a martingale, which was tied to the front of the saddle to keep it from slipping back during uphill travel, this ornament served no utilitarian purpose.

Sioux saddle blanket, circa 1890. 8530

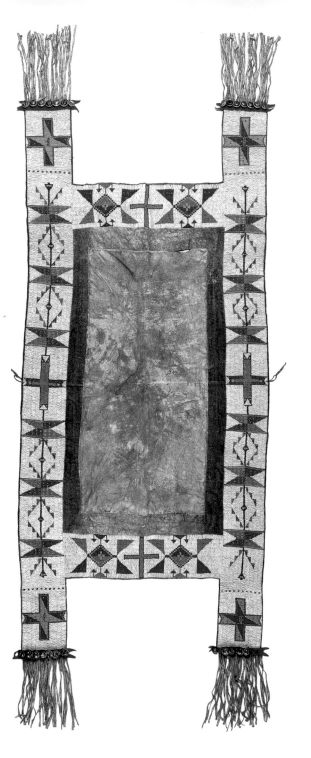

A SONG FOR THE HORSE NATION

Chiricahua Apache saddle bag, circa 1880s. 2/1200

The crimson cloth backing the cutouts is a wool fabric that was widely traded in the nineteenth century and was known, appropriately enough, as trade cloth.

Absaroke (Crow) horse crupper, circa 1885. 2/3106

The Crow created beadwork in a range of styles, from geometric to floral abstractions. The smaller end of this crupper would have been tied to the saddle, and the hanging tabs, with their metal jingles, would have provided a nice sound as they swayed. Early observers described Crow camps on the move as perhaps more beautiful and lively than any others.

This saddle blanket is decorated with pony beads. Pony beads were among the first glass beads introduced to Native Americans through trade with Europeans. Beaded on buffalo hide, this piece is important as much for its age as for its simple and elegant geometric design, typical of that period. While most of today's bead workers prefer to work with seed beads, the women of some Plateau tribes still wear dresses decorated with the larger pony beads.

Lakota hoof ornaments, late 19th century.
2/9627

Many Plains tribes made hoof covers.
Not intended for everyday use, hoof
covers such as these were strictly
decorative, brought out only for
parades and celebrations.

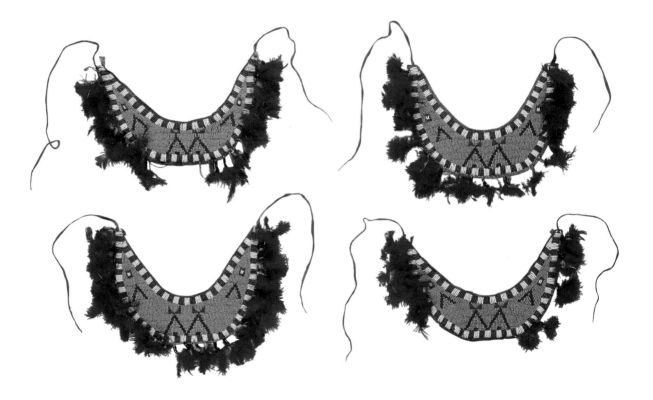

East or Woods Cree saddlecloth, circa 1885. Canada. 11/3506

The uncommon shape of this beautiful beaded saddlecloth may have been adapted from that of U.S. Cavalry blankets. The compact floral beadwork at each of the lobed corners is similar to the decoration on the Cree pad saddle shown on page 32. This blanket also is unusual because none of the designs on the four corners match.

Seneca farmers harvesting and hauling hay in a horse-drawn wagon, July 1941. Cattaraugus Reservation, New York. P19954

Gerry Jones (Seneca) and his family, circa 1900. Cattaraugus Reservation, New York. N23086

Horse and sled caravan on the trail to
Mistassini River, 1926. Quebec, Canada.
Photograph by Frank G. Speck. N11829

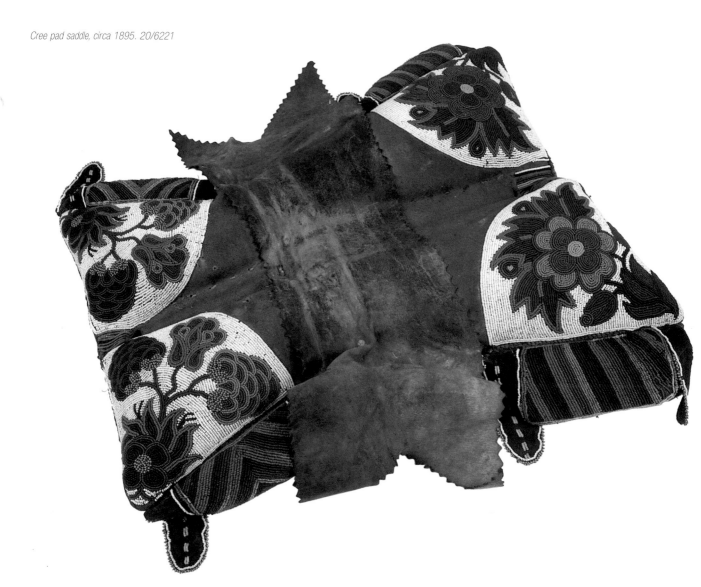

Prairie Cree pad saddle, circa 1910.
Canada. 14/7956

Often stuffed with buffalo hair, pad saddles
were used extensively by Plains Indians
during battles or for racing and hunting.
Fully decorated pad saddles such as this
one, however, were usually saved for
parades or traded for other goods. The
decorative border, made of bands of color,
is a common Cree style.

Possibly Cree bridle, late 19th century.
13/2358

This simple, understated design is made somewhat unusual by its use of bells, which would have made a nice sound as the horse moved. The artist may have been Plains Cree or from a neighboring tribe.

Absaroke (Crow) horse head ornament, circa 1890. Montana. 12/6404

This bridle is Spanish in style, with its distinctively shaped bit and chain embellishment that would have dangled below the horse's chin.

At the Crow Fair parade every year, many families still display old horse ornaments such as this one, and what they don't already have, they make. An elderly Crow woman once explained, "We are show people. If we've got it, we bring it out and show it."

This old-fashioned and simple approach to fastening a bridle involves inserting rope into the horse's mouth between the teeth, then looping and tying the remainder of the length of rope around the head to form one rein. The little girl in back has been bound onto the horse to ensure she doesn't fall.

HORSE EQUIPMENT

It is said that some Indian riders long ago didn't always use bridles but guided their ponies by applying pressure to the horse's ribs with their knees. A well-trained mount could quickly respond. Another method of not only guiding the horse but also of leading it was the use of a buffalo-hair braided rope that, when inserted into the natural gap in the horse's teeth and tied under the jaw, formed a basic bridle. Later, Spanish-style bridles were adopted, although the bit caused the horse more pain. Beaded strips over the harness leather added an Indian flavor to these bridles. By the nineteenth century, the gear utilized by Plains riders varied somewhat, but some basic necessities made life easier.

A bridle and saddle of some type completed the basic equestrian paraphernalia, and a rider had many options. He or she could sit on a horse's bare back—appropriately called bareback riding—or use a rawhide-covered wood-and-bone framework saddle with a high pommel (a knob on the front of the saddle) and high cantle (rear of the saddle) for stability.

There was also the less-inhibiting pad saddle and various versions of the white man's saddle. Occasionally, a crupper (a wide, decorated strap) was tied onto the rear of the saddle and under the horse's tail to keep the saddle from tipping forward.

Cree or Métis quirt, circa 1865. 3/2875

Another important accessory was the quirt. Similar in purpose to a riding crop, a quirt is a small whip used to urge the animal onward at a faster pace. It also adds a certain flair to the rider's appearance. Plains Indian quirts were often made from pieces of elk horn or a bone that had been decorated with carving, incising, or sometimes paint. The handle of the quirt could be fashioned from carved wood or a short length of naturally shaped willow or brush. Strips of leather were fastened to the bottom, and a leather wrist strap was often firmly attached to the main body of the quirt and looped over the hand and around the wrist so that the quirt could not be dropped.

In addition to their usefulness in stinging a horse's rump, quirts could be used to count coup in battle. Counting coup, an important ritual of Plains warfare, entailed touching the enemy ceremonially but not killing him and was an indication of great bravery and a cause for honor. Although the use of a quirt to count coup would not be lethal to an enemy, it would probably distract his attention long enough for the warrior to depart safely.

—George P. Horse Capture (A'aninin)

Possibly Assiniboine quirt, circa 1870s.
19/5092

Although it is easy to forget, we must remember that American Indians have lived on this continent for tens of thousands of years, and their imprint can be seen across the landscape. Prehistoric drawings and carvings—the earliest of art forms—decorate the walls of cliffs and caves across North America and tell us of spiritual journeys, supernatural beings, animals, and the exploits of warriors from long ago. By identifying stylistic motifs, scholars can often determine which groups created the drawings, and occasionally, a match can be found by comparing figures in rock art to those items made by contemporary tribes, confirming that some ancient art styles reach across the centuries.

A wedge-shaped anthropomorphic figure carved into a stone wall in southern Alberta, Canada, is similar to the one incised into the handle of this quirt, collected in the early twentieth century. Both works could have been made by the Assiniboine people, although the style of beadwork on the quirt's strap is more typical of Prairie tribes.

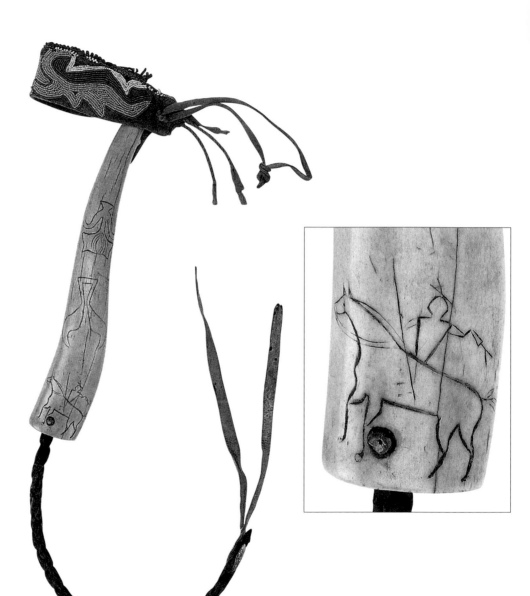

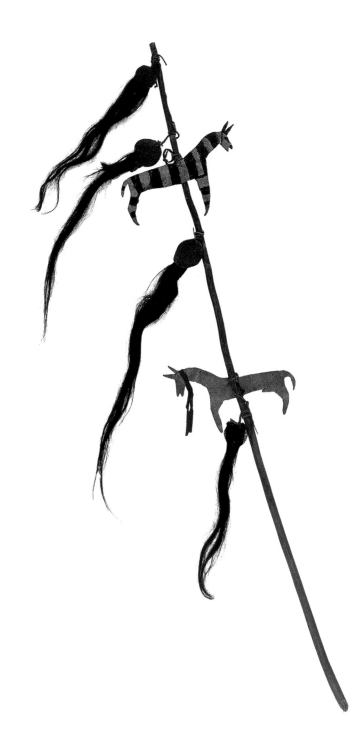

Piikuni (Blackfeet) coup stick, late 19th century. 14/9565

In the buffalo days of the mid-1800s, age-graded warrior societies were vital to the survival of Plains tribes. One way a Plains warrior demonstrated his bravery was by "counting coup," that is, galloping up to an enemy and touching him, sometimes with a special stick made for that purpose, instead of killing him. Coup sticks were also carried in ceremonial dances, during which warriors related stories of their courage and daring.

The rawhide horses attached to this coup stick represent the horses its owner rode in battle, and the hair locks are scalp replicas, made by attaching hair from a horse's tail to a piece of cloth or rawhide and painting it red.

High Wolf.

Nez Perces.

Yellow Nose (Ute, raised as Cheyenne),
Portrait of High Wolf, *circa 1880.*
23/4368

This drawing shows High Wolf counting
coup with a riding quirt against a Nez
Perce. The imitation scalp under his
horse's chin indicates the accomplish-
ments of both horse and rider.

Horse Society

There is among the Teton Sioux an organization called the Horse Society. It was said that some of the songs in the following group were used in this society and were also used on the warpath to make a horse swift and sure. The estimation in which the horse is held by the Sioux is shown by a speech by Brave Buffalo. This speech was made before the singing of his first song and was recorded by the phonograph. Freely translated it is as follows:

> Of all the animals the horse is the best friend of the Indian, for without it he could not go on long journeys. A horse is the Indian's most valuable piece of property. If an Indian wishes to gain something, he promises his horse that if the horse will help him, he will paint it with native dye, that all may see that help has come to him through the aid of his horse.

Śiya´ka said that on one occasion when he was hard pressed on the warpath, he dismounted, and, standing in front of his horse, spoke to him, saying:

> We are in danger. Obey me promptly that we may conquer. If you have to run for your life and mine, do your best, and if we reach home, I will give you the best eagle feather I can get and the finest *sina´ lu´ ta*, and you shall be painted with the best paint.*

*The eagle feather was tied to the horse's tail, and the *sina´ lu´ ta* was a strip of red cloth fastened around the horse's neck.

MY HORSE FLIES LIKE A BIRD
kola´
mita´ śuŋ ke
kiŋyaŋ´ yaŋ
iŋ´ yaŋke lo

friend
my horse
flies like a bird
as it runs

—Sung by Brave Buffalo

If a young man had been successful on his first war party, it was expected that at the first large gathering after his return, he would give away many horses and receive his manhood name, suggestive of his deed of valor. After that, he discarded his childhood or boyhood names. If he went on the warpath again and excelled his first achievement, on his return, he could be given still another name to correspond with his second victory.

A man who captured horses usually gave some of them to the women of his family. This custom is expressed in the first song below:

HORSES I AM BRINGING

taŋke´	older sister
hina´ pa yo	come outside
śuŋka´ wakaŋ	horses
awa´ kuwe	I am bringing back

taŋke´	older sister
hina´ piŋ	come outside
na	and
waŋźi´ oyus´ payo	you may catch one of them

—Sung by Two Shields

HORSES ARE COMING

tate´ oü´ ye to´pa kiŋ	the four winds are blowing
śuŋka´wakaŋ waŋzig´ źi	some horses
aü´ welo´	are coming

—Sung by Brave Buffalo

WHEN A HORSE NEIGHS

aŋ´ paö	daybreak
hina´ pe	appears
ćiŋhaŋ´	when
śunka´ kaŋ waŋ	a horse
hotoŋ´ we	neighs

·---Sung by Brave Buffalo

WATCH YOUR HORSES

Kaŋǵi´ wića´ śa	Crow Indian
kiŋ suŋk awaŋ´ glaka po	you must watch your horses
suŋ´ ka wama´ noŋ	a horse thief
sa	often
miye´ yelo´	am I

—Sung by Two Shields

[Text and song translations by Frances Densmore]

Meeting of the Blackfeet Little Dog Society, circa 1903. Montana. Photograph by Fred R. Meyer. N21868

This photograph reveals warrior society material even on the tipi, with its depictions of guns, hatchets, and war exploits. Unlike many Plains tribes, the Blackfeet have continued to use early, more traditional tipi designs such as these.

*Holds the Enemy (Absaroke [Crow])
on horseback, circa 1905. Montana.
Photograph by Fred E. Miller. N13767*

In contrast to Spotted Rabbit (opposite),
who is dressed more for show, Holds the
Enemy looks every part the warrior, with
his war shirt and impressive bonnet.

*White Bull (Sioux) on horseback.
Photograph by the O'Neill Photo
Company. P14287*

Possibly Chief Joseph White Bull
(Minniconjou Sioux), who has sometimes
been credited with slaying Lieutenant
Colonel George Armstrong Custer at Little
Bighorn, Montana, on June 25, 1876.
If this is indeed White Bull, the handwritten
caption, which reads "first friendly Indian
to visit whites in Custer S.D.," has
unintended irony.

"WHITE BULL" FIRST FRIENDLY INDIAN
TO VISIT WHITES IN CUSTER, S.D.   -41-
O'NEILL PHOTO CO.

Spotted Rabbit (Absaroke [Crow]) on horseback, circa 1905. Montana. Photograph by Fred E. Miller. N13766

Note Spotted Rabbit's elaborate accoutrements: the horse head ornament, martingale, mountain lion–skin saddle blanket, beaded stirrups, blanket strip, and feather duster (probably a trade item). His lance is probably a warrior society item.

Possibly Chief Eagle of the Salish (at right), with an unidentified woman on horseback, circa 1905. St. Ignatius, Montana, on the Flathead Reservation. P12780

Kainah (Blood) man with horse, 1882. Photograph by Daniel Cadzow. P1531

This man is wearing a Hudson's Bay blanket, a trade item made in England that the Kainah, Blackfeet, and Métis restyled into coats known as capotes. The blankets usually had a yellowish background, with stripes of black, green, yellow, and red. This example, with its three black stripes, indicates that its trade worth was three pelts.

Horse Images in Everyday Life

Lakota quilled bag, circa 1870s. 8934

Plains Indian artists depict horses in all media, from paint and beadwork to carvings in wood and stone. This bag is embroidered with dyed porcupine quills, a traditional technique that was nearly lost to the widespread availability of trade beads in the nineteenth century. Quillwork has made a comeback in the last few decades, however, and a number of gifted artists are again creating in this medium.

Central Plains (possibly Oto or Kaw)
beaded leggings. Oklahoma. 2/960

A SONG FOR THE HORSE NATION

Central Plains (possibly Oto or Potawatomi) beaded cloth coat, circa 1895. Oklahoma. 2/972

The designs on this coat are associated with a short-lived religious movement that centered on the ceremonial uprooting and replanting of a cedar tree. Bison skulls (beaded onto the coat's breast, just below the cedar roots, as well as around the hem) were important to the ceremony, which also involved six riders. Like many similar religions that swept Indian tribes during the early 1890s, the movement, which was based on a vision of the prophet William Faw Faw (Oto), instructed its followers to renounce European and American influences and return to traditional ways.

Possibly Piikuni (Blackfeet) muslin dress with painted decoration, circa 1875. 17/6078

Records indicate that this dress is Blackfeet, but considering the style, this seems unlikely. The paintings on this dress, which appear to depict vignettes of intertribal warfare between northern and southern Plains groups, recall the distinctions—in battle and on horse raids—of one individual and indicate that he suffered five wounds. To wear a dress such as this would have been an honor reserved for a close family member, possibly the wife or sister of the warrior depicted.

Cheyenne shirt, circa 1865. 8/8034

Shirts such as these were made and worn by esteemed Plains warriors, spiritual leaders, and diplomats. Many of the locks on this shirt are horsehair, and the shirt's owner is probably the lance-bearing warrior on the yellow horse. The zigzag line running from the horse's head and down its front leg symbolizes lightning; it would have been painted on the horse to provide it with power in battle.

Shirt owned by Sinte Gleska (Spotted Tail, Brulé Lakota), circa 1853. 17/6694

Sinte Gleska (1823?–81) was a warrior, a prisoner, a peace delegate, and an advocate for educating his people in places other than government- or church-sponsored boarding schools. Sinte Gleska University, the first tribal college on the Rosebud Indian Reservation, honors him today.

This shirt, which he earned as a young warrior, is decorated with more than a hundred locks of hair, representing coups, scalps, and captured horses. The hair on many warrior shirts is also frequently from family or cherished horses, because to carry a lock of hair was to hold some of the power from its source.

The quillwork here was made by using a rare technique known as Spotted Tail quillwork—a reference to this shirt, which is its premier example. Very attractive and difficult, the technique hasn't survived. Also unusual is the shirt's design, with strips of medallions down the arms.

Sinte Gleska (Brulé Lakota, 1823?–81). P20494

Chaticksi (Pawnee) coat belonging to Lone Wolf (back view), circa 1910. 19/3199

This Western-style tailored coat reflects the influence of the white world on Plains culture in its straight body, even hem, and collar, as well as in its decorative use of five-pointed stars and crosses. The two-toned speckled horse with the horn on its forehead could represent a painted horse or possibly a spirit horse dreamed by Lone Wolf.

Lakota beaded hide coat, circa 1890.
8848

As European and Native cultures met, new styles developed. This Western-cut hide jacket is beaded with pictographic figures, but instead of illustrating an individual's exploits, as pictographs typically do, these images are simply used as decoration. The horses' tails are doubled and tied in preparation for battle.

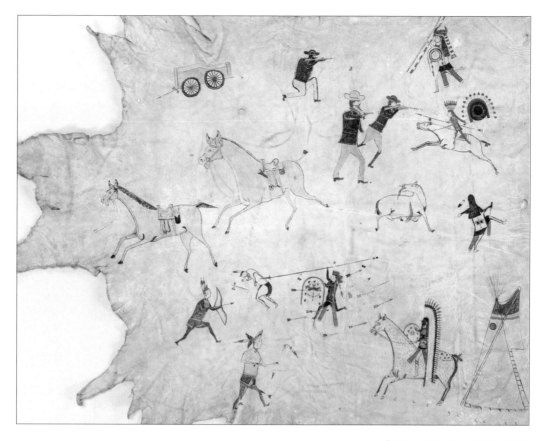

Comanche hide robe, mid-19th century.
2/2169

Oral traditions were frequently documented on hide robes; the main actions usually read from left to right. Depicting Comanche warriors fighting U.S. Cavalry and enemy tribes, this robe records, in typical southern Plains style, a great conflict. The central figure in the fur turban is probably the artist; not surprisingly, he is winning the battle.

Taos Pueblo buffalo hide robe. 5/719

The horse figures painted on this robe have thick bodies and short, straight legs, which distinguish them from the more elongated, sleeker horses typical of the Plains style. All are pintos, which is also unusual.

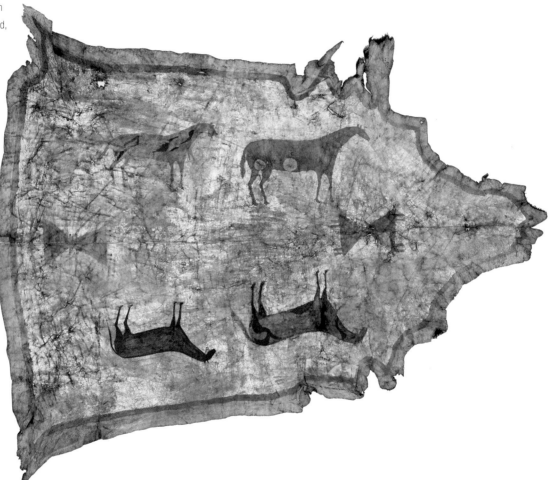

Piikuni (Blackfeet) elkskin robe with painted decoration by Mountain Chief, mid 19th century. Montana. 22/1878

Unique for its use of color, the paintings on this robe suggest a very complicated vignette. The Blackfeet are encountering two different enemies—other tribes and bears (the latter seen in the lower left corner)—and are holding their own. The small arcs represent hoof marks, and the arrowlike marks below them indicate the direction in which the horses were headed.

Yakama beaded bag, circa 1910.
14/9415

Walla Walla beaded bag, circa 1915.
6/5436

The Indian people of the Plateau have a long artistic history of weaving cornhusk bags, and, after trade goods became widely available, they made cloth bags decorated with glass beads. This one features a man astride a prancing horse, wearing what appears to be the Army uniform of a corporal.

Cheyenne River Sioux
beaded tipi bag, circa 1885. 6/325

The pictograph on this tipi bag tells a story in much the same way that more elaborate robes and warrior shirts do, although in a more abbreviated fashion. Our hero has stolen a number of horses and possibly a wife as well. The three black-and-brown pipes indicate that he led a war party on three occasions, and the heads represent enemies he killed. Brown, blue, pink, and yellow are used to suggest that the horses are of many colors.

The Art of Capturing Horses

JOE MEDICINE CROW COUNTS
COUP DURING WORLD WAR II

Capturing a prize horse from an enemy was the dream of every aspiring Plains Indian warrior. Young men risked their lives to sneak into an enemy village and leave riding a splendid war horse that had been tethered next to its owner's tipi. The successful horse thief had every right to boast about his exploit for the rest of his life, and, lest anyone forget, he might depict it in a pictograph drawing on his tipi cover, he might wear beaded vests or shirts featuring the horse he had captured, or he might carve a wooden effigy that he would hold as he danced in an honor ceremony or participated in other important community events. As can be seen from the many artistic expressions in this book, symbols of horses could be incorporated into everything from tent pegs to clothing to flutes to pipe bowls.

These traditions have survived even into the twenty-first century. Nowhere is this more evident than on the Crow Reservation in southeastern Montana, the home of the Crow Indians, a people who still cherish their horses and their warrior tradition—as I learned from my adopted brother, Dr. Joseph Medicine Crow, now in his nineties. Joe, who has an honorary doctorate from the University of Montana, grew up listening to the stories of his grandfather White Man Runs Him and the other aged veterans of the Indian wars. Thanks to World War II, Joe got the chance to capture his own horse in the finest tradition of a Plains Indian warrior.

Near the end of the war, the Germans were retreating on all fronts. One night, Joe recalls, his platoon was following a group of S.S. officers on horseback. The U.S. soldiers could hear the clop, clop of the hooves ahead of them on the asphalt road. Near daybreak, the horsemen went to a farm down a dirt road, where they planned to hide. "We followed their trail in the moonlight and arrived at a villa. We came there and found a little pasture with a barn."

The commanding officer sat down with the platoon leaders to discuss how best to handle the situation. Joe recalls, "All I could think about was those horses in the paddock." Joe mentioned the horses to his commanding officer.

> I said, "Maybe I should get those horses out of the corral before you attack because some of those S.S. guys might be able to escape on them. It would only take me about five minutes." The C.O. looked at me funny for a second, but he probably had an idea of what I was up to. I was the only Indian in the outfit, and he always called me "Chief." He said, "Okay, Chief, you're on." That's all I needed. I took one

of my buddies and we sneaked down toward the corral and the barn. Nothing was moving. The horses were tired, just standing around. I crawled through the paddock fence and came up to one of them. I told him, "Whoa. Whoa." He snorted a little bit, but settled down. I had this little rope with me that I used to tie my blanket. It was about six feet long. I tied a loop around his lower jaw like the old-time Crow warriors used to do, and then I tried to get on, but it was a tall horse, and my boots were so muddy and caked up, I couldn't do it. Finally, I led the horse to the watering trough and stood on that to get on its back.

Meanwhile, I told my buddy that I was going to the other end of the paddock behind the horses. "As soon as I get there," I said, "I will give a little whistle, and when I do, you open the gate and get out of the way." Well, I got back there, gave the whistle, then a war whoop, and started the horses moving. The kid took off and here they come.

Just about that time, our boys opened fire on the farmhouse. There was lots of commotion. I just took off. There was some timber about a half-mile away, so I just headed that way. By that time it was daylight, so as we galloped along, I looked at the horses. I had about forty or fifty head. I was riding a sorrel with a blaze, a real nice horse. So I did something spontaneously: I sang a Crow praise song. I sang this song a little bit and rode around the horses. The horses looked at me. Finally, I left them in the woods, but I stayed on my horse and headed back to the farmhouse. The firing had stopped by now; the Germans had surrendered real quick. So I came back.

After we finished mopping up, the company commander said, "Let's go," and we took off. There was a gravel railroad bed nearby, which made the walking a little better. As the guys took off down the railroad track, I was still on my horse. It was good, better to ride than walk, so I just stayed on the horse about a mile. Finally, the C.O. said, "Chief, you better get off. You make too good a target." When I got back to the Crow Reservation after the war, the elders gave me credit for that coup just like it was done in the old days.

Such exploits continue to fire the imaginations of later generations of Crow soldiers. Carson Walks Over Ice, Joe's nephew, fought in Vietnam as a Green Beret. His goal, too, was to count coup on the enemy, and he did so many times, but to his regret, he never got a horse. "I did get two elephants, and that should have counted for something," he says, "but the elders did not see it my way."

—Herman J. Viola

Old Buffalo's War Narrative

In August 1913, Old Buffalo (Tataŋk´-ehaŋ´ni), with Swift Dog, came to McLaughlin, South Dakota, to confer with [Frances Densmore]. They regarded this conference very seriously. Old Buffalo said, "We come to you as from the dead. The things about which you ask us have been dead to us for many years. In bringing them to our minds, we are calling them from the dead, and when we have told you about them, they will go back to the dead, to remain forever."

Old Buffalo was born in the year 1845, designated in the Sioux picture calendar, "winter in which lodges with roofs were built." When he was twenty-eight years old, he led a war party against the Crows. On this expedition, he and his comrades were entirely surrounded by the Crows, an event which Old Buffalo depicted in a drawing. Old Buffalo said that at the time of this expedition, his band of the Sioux were living in the "Queen's Land" (Canada), but had come down to the United States on a buffalo hunt. From this temporary camp, the expedition started under his leadership. Old Buffalo said further:

> One night, the Crows came and stole our horses. I had an older sister of whom I was very fond. The Crows stole her horse and she cried a long time. This made my heart very bad. I said, "I will go and pay them back." A friend said that he would go with me. I said to my friend, "We will go and look for the Crows. Wherever their horses are corralled, we will find them." Eleven others went with us, so there were thirteen in the party, and I was the leader. It was in the coldest part of the winter, the moon called by the Sioux Caŋ napo´pa wi, "Wood-cracking moon." The snow was deep, and I am lame in one leg, but I was angry, and I went. I thought, "Even if I die, I will be content." The women made warm clothing and moccasins for us to wear, and we started away. We carried no shelter. When night came, we shoveled aside the snow and laid down brush, on which we slept. At the fork of the Missouri River, we took the eastern branch and followed its course. It was eleven nights from the fork of the river to the enemy's camp, and every night we sang this song. It is one of the "wolf songs."

SONG OF SELF-RELIANCE

eya´
miśeya´ tuwa´ ćaŋte´
kaćaś´
ećiŋ´
śuŋk owa´ le

well
I depend upon no one's heart (or courage) but my own
so
thinking this
I look for horses

—Sung by Old Buffalo

Old Buffalo continued:

As we neared the end of our journey, we were overtaken by a fearful blizzard. There was a butte in which we found a sheltered place and stayed for two days, as my leg was very painful. After the storm subsided, we looked around and could see the enemy's village. Night came again, but my leg was so painful that we rested another day. The next afternoon, as the sun was getting low, I tightened my belt and made ready for whatever might befall. We walked toward the enemy's village and entered a rocky country, like the Bad Lands. Then it was dark.

A great number of Crows were camped at this place, and there was dancing in two parts of the village. We were close to the village, but no one saw us; only the dogs barked. We went up to the edge of the village and got in where there were many horses in a bunch. We drove the herd before us and they trotted quietly along. After getting a safe distance from the camp, we mounted some of the horses and drove the rest before us. We did not stop, but kept the horses trotting fast all night. When daylight came, we counted the horses and found that there were fifty-three. All that day we traveled, and as the sun sank, we rested. We were tired, as we had no saddles, and that night, we slept.

The next morning, there came another terrible blizzard. My eyelashes were frozen so that I could scarcely see. I went back a little distance to see if we were being followed, then I returned to my companions. I had realized that the tracks of the horses made a trail and I saw that the enemy were pursuing us. This was my war party and I felt a great responsibility for its safety.

The Crows overtook us and secured most of the horses which we had captured from them. We jumped down a steep, rocky place, and soon we were entirely surrounded by the Crows. A Sioux boy, about fifteen years old, was with us, and he was shot in the back. We fought as long as the sun moved in the sky. It was a hard struggle. Every time we fired a gun, it turned white with frost.

The Crows took the saddles from their horses and charged back at us, but our fire was more than they could stand, and they finally retreated, leaving their saddles on the ground. We captured these saddles and took them back to the place where we were first overtaken by the Crows. There we found only four horses alive. We put one of the captured saddles on a horse and lifted the wounded boy to the horse's back. I held the reins and walked beside the horse all that night. When daylight came, we rested. The boy had no pillow, so I lay down and he laid his head on my body. There was timber near the place, and the next day, we made a travois for the boy, and I rode the horse that dragged it. That night, we traveled on, and about midnight, we reached a certain place and made a camp. We had occasionally killed a buffalo for food, and as the men on foot had worn out their moccasins, we took fresh buffalo hide and tied it on their feet. The three horses ran away, but we caught them.

All the following night we traveled, and the next day, we were at the fork of the Missouri River, where we stayed two nights.

While we were on the warpath, our friends had finished their buffalo hunt and returned to Canada. I kept four men with me and the sick boy and sent the others home to make a report of the expedition. We kept the horses with us and followed slowly. The boy was thirsty, and as there was no cup, I took the hide of a buffalo head, put snow in it, and then put a hot stone in the snow. Thus, the boy had hot

Detail from Cheyenne River Sioux painted-hide shield cover, circa 1880s. (Entire shield is shown on page 70.)
6/2195

water to drink. He wanted soup, so I took the buffalo tripe and boiled meat in it. So the boy had soup.

We camped for a time beside a creek, and as we came near the "Queen's Land," we camped again. There, the father and mother of the boy met us. They had heard the news from the other members of the party and started at once to meet us. After we had given the boy to his parents, we went on with the horses, leaving them to travel more slowly. It was dark when we reached home, and we fired our guns to let the people know of our coming. The next day, the boy arrived. For two days and nights, I stayed with him constantly. I did this because I felt myself to be the cause of his misfortune. The boy had come to call me "father," and at the end of this time, he said, "Father, you can go home now to your own lodge." I went to my own lodge and slept that night. The next morning, the boy died. He is always spoken of as Wana´gli ya´ku, "Brings the arrow," because he brought home the arrow in his body.

I did not keep any of the horses for myself, because I was the leader of the war party.

In describing another exploit, Old Buffalo said, "On our expedition, we sang this song, hoping that we would capture many horses,"

I LOOK FOR THEM

Kaŋgi´ wića´ śa kiŋ
owi´ ćawale
iye´ waya
ća
taśuŋ´ ke kiŋ
awa´ kuwe

the Crow Indians
I look for them
I found them
so
their horses
I brought home

—Sung by Old Buffalo

Old Buffalo concluded:

We found the direction in which the Crows were traveling, went around, and headed them off. It was almost dark when we approached their village. They were camped in a circle. The afterglow was still in the sky, and this light was in back of us as we went up a little creek from that direction toward the village. We could see the cooking fires. We were on horseback and we lay flat on our horses, leaning close to the horses' heads. So we crept near to their horses.

When we stepped among the horses, one of them snorted at a stranger. Then the Crows came with their guns. They had seen us, though we did not know it. My eyes were only for the horses. They began firing, and before I had a chance to get away, my horse was shot. I snatched the reins and pulled, but the horse's jaw was broken. I went on. They shot again and he fell. I jumped as he went down. The man who went with me ran away at the first attack and left me alone. I ran ahead, and as the Crows were loading their guns, I dodged from one shelter to another. They kept firing in the direction I had started to go.

The young man who ran away saw me. He was in a safe place and he shouted, "Come this way." He was on horseback, and we sat double on his horse. We traveled some distance and came to the creek by which we had approached the Crow camp. We stayed at the creek that night. The Crows broke camp, and late the next day, we went back to the deserted ground. There lay my horse, dead. We examined the horse and found that his shoulder was broken. My oldest sister had raised that horse.

We went back to the creek and stayed that night. The Sioux were moving to their last camp of the year, and there we joined them.

Detail from Cheyenne River Sioux painted-hide shield cover, circa 1880s. (Entire shield is shown on page 70.) 6/2195

[Narrative and translations by Frances Densmore]

I WOULD STEAL HORSES

I would steal horses
for you, if there were any left,
give a dozen of the best
to your father, the auto mechanic

in the small town where you were born
and where he will die in the dark.
I am afraid of his hands, which have
rebuilt more of the small parts

of this world than I ever will.
I would offer my sovereignty, take
every promise as your final lie, the last
point before we start refusing the exact.

I would wrap us both in old blankets
hold every disease tight against our skin.

—Sherman Alexie (Spokane/Coeur d'Alene)

Hunkpapa Lakota dance stick, circa 1899. 20/1294

This dance club would have been carried in horse dances. Decorated with brass hawk bells, golden-eagle feathers, and imitation scalps, it depicts a cherished horse—possibly a pinto—that suffered two bullet holes to the neck.

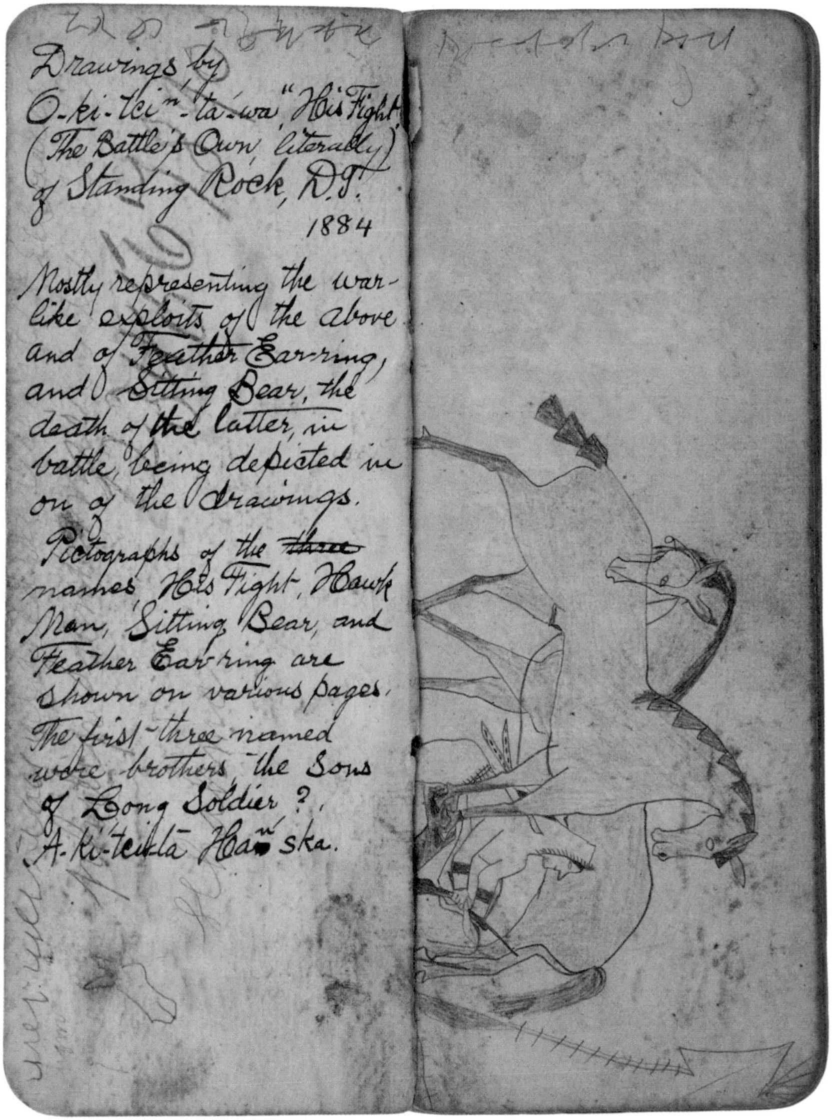

Drawings by
O-ki-tci'''-ta-wa, "His Fight"
(The Battle's Own literally)
of Standing Rock, D.T.
1884

Mostly representing the war-
like exploits of the above
and of Feather Earring,
and Sitting Bear, the
death of the latter, in
battle, being depicted in
one of the drawings.
Pictographs of the three
names His Fight, Hawk
Man, Sitting Bear, and
Feather Ear-ring are
shown on various pages.
The first three named
were brothers the Sons
of Long Soldier ?.
A-ki-tcikta Hanska.

Cheyenne River Sioux painted-hide shield cover, circa 1880s. 6/2195

This shield cover records a battle scene between the Lakota and some of their enemies, possibly Crow or Pawnee, who are recognizable by the topknot hairstyle that was popular with both tribes. The hero/owner of this shield, wearing a split-horn war bonnet, is at the center, moving left.

Most tribes use drums of some sort to provide rhythm or ambience to their singing, dancing, or prayers. The Plains tribes followed the buffalo for their sustenance, so everything in their world had to be useful and easily transportable. Their drums, such as this one, were small and could serve as a medium for artwork. Here, a lance-carrying warrior, ready for battle, sits astride a pinto pony whose tail is tied up with a red wool strip. This drum is unusual because it's painted on the inside. The outside is painted red, a color often used for sacred or important objects.

A WARRIOR, TO HIS HORSE

My horse be swift in flight
Even like a bird;
My horse be swift in flight,
Bear me now in safety
Far from the enemy's arrows,
And you shall be rewarded
With streamers and ribbons red.

—Lone Man (Sioux)

[Translated by Frances Densmore]

*Dance stick owned by No Two Horns
(Teton Lakota). North Dakota. 14/1566*

We can learn something about No Two
Horns' horse by examining the details of
this dance stick—probably the most
famous and widely copied dance stick—
which was created to honor it. The red
triangles indicate this horse's wounds,
and the scalp replica may pay additional
homage to the horse, or it may testify to
No Two Horns' own exploits. Although it
was suffering from six different wounds,
the horse managed to carry No Two
Horns to victory. The eagle feather and
fancy silver bridle also suggest the
importance of this animal and show that
it was a cherished companion. The carved
hoof at the bottom of the stick and the
rawhide ears add interesting elements
as well.

Assiniboine horse stick. Made by Medicine Bear, circa 1860. 11/8044

Most successful warriors had special relationships with their favorite horses because they depended upon each other. In order to confirm and continue this close bond, a warrior would often immortalize a horse that had saved his life by creating a wood carving in the horse's image.

The famous warrior and diplomat Medicine Bear carved this likeness in memory of his war pony, killed in battle in northern Montana in the mid-1800s; the mane and tail on this dance stick came from that pony. Today, Medicine Bear himself is remembered by a social center named in his honor on the Fort Belknap Indian Reservation in Montana.

Ioway (Iowa) horse-effigy mirror board,
circa 1880. 14/805

Europeans frequently traded small glass
mirrors to Indians. Plains Indians wore
them on their fur chest decorations or
inserted them into wooden frames, which
they carved into different shapes, including
those of animals. Often, they ornamented
the frames with brass tacks (another
popular trade item), metal inlay, or paint.
The heart-shaped cutout is a decorative
element, and the inlay is made of lead.
Men carried mirrors such as this
in dances.

Ho Chunk (Winnebago) carved wood sash heddle, circa 1862. Nebraska. 23/8761

Small heddles such as this one were used in weaving to separate and guide the warp threads.

Diné (Navajo) beeldléí *(blanket), circa 1875. 24/2373*

The Diné, or Navajo, people are famous for their beautiful blankets, which were sought after by many Native groups long before trade began with Europeans.

*Diné (Navajo) textile, late 19th century.
New Mexico. 14/5896*

Mayo Indians on horseback, 1924. San Jose, Sonora, Mexico. Photograph by Edward H. Davis. N24756

Yaqui man on horseback, 1922. Vicam, Sonora, Mexico. Photograph by Edward H. Davis. P3740

Ysidro Nejo (Kumeyaay [Diegueño]) on horseback, 1923. Mesa Grande, California. Photograph by Edward H. Davis. N24317

Navajo women at the Gallup Ceremonial, circa 1940. Gallup, New Mexico. Photograph by Rolf Tietgens. Lot 179

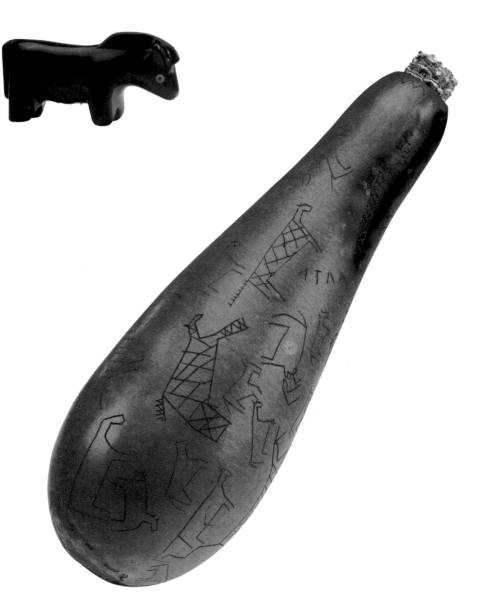

Zuni figurine, mid-20th century. 25/6124

Traditionally, fetish carvings were, and are, given as gifts. Kept in the home to represent the six directions, Zuni fetishes are still used in a ceremonial context today. The fetish carving is believed to be a source of protection, keeping harm from its owner while also attracting good fortune. Fetishes are occasionally used by livestock owners to bring good health and good fortune to their animals, but this fetish was probably made for sale, as horses play a lesser role in Zuni culture. Many carvings are now marketed to tourists, who wear them as talismans in the hope that they will bring any number of attributes, including good luck, strength, and courage.
—Miranda Belarde-Lewis (Zuni/Tlingit)

Lengua gourd medicine container,
20th century. Paraguay. 14/621

Dating from the pre-Columbian era, gourd engraving is one of the most ancient and uninterrupted indigenous traditions in the Western Hemisphere. This piece, made by the Lengua group of the Chaco region of South America, has incised decoration depicting stylized horses and plants. It would have been used as a container for medicine in either liquid or powder form.

A SONG FOR THE HORSE NATION

Wooden qero *(ritual cup), 17th century. Colonial Peru. 10/5635*

Produced in pairs, qeros are vessels used in the ritual consumption of maize beer. They have been made by the Native peoples of the Andean region of South America for millennia. This one, carved from the trunk of a tree and decorated with paint made from plant resin, depicts a man on horseback, wearing European-style clothing.

Possibly Piikuni (Blackfeet) flute, circa 1890s. Montana. 14/3392

Courting rituals were very important in many Native American cultures, and flutes were often used by young Plains men for purposes of courting. Records indicate that this flute is Blackfeet in origin, but it may have been made by one of the Prairie tribes, who are better known for this style of work.

Possibly Cheyenne River Sioux pipe bag, circa 1890. 1/3949

Many Native cultures use tobacco for prayers during ceremonies; pipe bags such as this one were made by Plains Indians to carry their pipes and tobacco. A portrait of a woman is beaded, appliqué-style, on the front of this bag. This is unusual and may indicate that she was a warrior. Elk-tooth dresses such as the one she wears suggest wealth and beauty.

There is almost certainly an interesting story behind this piece, although, unfortunately, it has been lost over time.

Probably Sioux catlinite pipe bowl with quilled stem, circa 1870. 3/3728

According to collection records, this pipe may be Sisseton Dakota, but its style suggests that it could also have been made by tribes located farther west.

Sioux wooden pipe tamper, late 19th century. 15/4760

Among many tribes, one of the most sacred ways to pray is through a ceremony centered on the smoking of a pipe. After the ceremonial accoutrements are carefully laid out, the pipe stem is inserted into the bowl, and the whole pipe is smudged, or cleansed, in sage smoke. Tobacco is placed into the pipe bowl and tucked in with a pipe tamper, and the pipe is then lighted and smoked by each of the participants as they pray. What better icon to decorate the tamper than the horse?

Fox knife. Iowa. Photograph by NMAI Photo Services staff. 16/6898

Metal knives with curved blades—called crooked, or canoe, knives—were among the first European-made tools to reach the tribes of the North American interior. The knives were used mainly to shape bowls and spoons from knots cut out of trees. Evidence suggests that before the arrival of metal tools, beaver teeth were sometimes chosen for this kind of woodwork.

The drawing contains the following handwritten captions:

"Poor Wolf" Removes a party of three Sioux who has stolen his horses – overtakes them, kills two of the Sioux & recovers his horses.

"Poor Wolf" returns afoot after killing a Sioux and is now dancing and counting his "Coups."

Poor Wolf (2d chief of the Gros Ventres) shooting into a Sioux lodge near Fort Sully, where he kills two Sioux

"Poor Wolf" dresses up, to administer justice to the abductor of his brother's wife, whom he catches, and gives a severe whipping to.

"Poor Wolf" killing a buffalo cow, and gives his entire equipments to the first man who comes to him, because his heart feels good"

4 2446A

Pictographic drawing. Artist unknown (Hidatsa), Exploits of Poor Wolf, Hidatsa Second Chief, *probably early 20th century. 4/2446A*

Drawn by men from tribes across the Great Plains, pictographs illustrating battles, horse raids, and courtships sprang to life on hides, cloth, and in ledger books. In this drawing, Poor Wolf recounts stories of his own bravery.

Several details are of particular interest. In the upper left, Poor Wolf sports a military coat and saber, possibly secured through battle. The eagle feathers tied to the tail of his very elegant horse suggest that this was a highly prized animal, as does the fancy Spanish bridle with chain decoration. The decorations on Poor Wolf's body could be tattoos; European artists who visited tribes in this region in the early 1800s painted portraits of men with similar tattoos. Finally, in winter counts and ledger drawings, individuals and their horses are almost always shown in profile, making the portrayal in the upper right unusual for its direct, head-on perspective. Note how the horse's hoofs line up evenly.

Red Dog (Lakota), Portrait of Few Tails, *circa 1884. 20/6230A*

Fully decked out in warrior society accoutrements, Few Tails appears to be dressed for battle. Most portraits, like this one, incorporate stylized faces. Because each Plains warrior's shield was decorated differently, individuals or tribes were identified in artwork by their shield designs and clothing styles.

Western Apache (Nide) basketry jar, circa 1925. Arizona. 21/5350

Apache peoples began using horses in significant numbers in the 1630s, at first to increase the extent of their trading and raiding networks. Nearly three hundred years later, when this basket—with its depiction of three mounted riders—was made, horses were crucial to the Apaches' growing cattle industry.

Comanche doll, 20th century. 22/4820

Famous as skilled horsemen, the Comanche owned more mounts than any other tribe. This doll portrays a warrior dressed in buckskin and carrying a wooden lance with a bone point.

Assiniboine woman on horseback, 1926.
Northern Alberta, Canada. N11750

AFFINITY: MUSTANG

Tonight after the sounds of day
have given way
she stands beneath the moon,
a gray rock shining.
She matches the land,
belonging.

She has a dark calm face,
her hooves like black stone
belong to the earth
the way it used to be,
long grasses
as grass followed rain
or wind laid down the plains of fall
or in winter now when
her fur changes and becomes snow
or her belly hair turns
the color of red water willows
at the creek,
her legs black as trees.

These horses
almost a shadow,
broken.

When we walk together
in the tall grasses, I feel her
as if I am walking with mystery,
with beauty and fierce powers,
as if for a while we are the same animal
and remember each other from before.

Or sometimes I sit on earth
and watch the wind blow her mane and tail
and the waves of dry grasses
all one way
and it calls to mind
how I've come such a long way
through time
to find her.

Some days I sing to her
remembering the Kiowa man
who sang to cover the screams
of their ponies killed by the Americans
the songs I know in my sleep.

Some nights, hearing her outside,
I think that she is to earth
what I am to her,
belonging.

But last night it was her infant that died
after the kinship and movement
of so many months.
Tonight I sit on the straw
and watch as the milk streams from her nipples
to the ground. I clean her face.
I've come such a long way through time
to find her and
it is the first time
I have ever seen a horse cry.

Sing then, the wind says,
Sing.

—Linda Hogan (Chickasaw)

Absaroke (Crow) children on horseback, circa 1900. Photograph by Fred E. Miller. P4231

At parades today, Crow equestrians are still renowned for their elaborate clothes and horse trappings. All the horse trappings that appear in this photograph still appear at the annual fair at Crow Agency in Montana—and the sound of jingling spoons on the beaded cruppers can still be heard.

Sarsi woman on horseback in front of tipi, circa 1895. P13554

BLUE HORSES RUSH IN

For Chamisa Bah Edmo, who was born March 6, 1991

Before the birth, she moved and pushed inside her mother.
Her heart pounded quickly and we recognized the sound of horses running:

The thundering of hooves on the desert floor.

Her mother clenched her fists and gasped.
She moans ageless pain and pushes: This is it!

Chamisa slips out, glistening wet and takes her first breath.

The wind outside swirls small leaves
and branches in the dark.

Her father's eyes are wet with gratitude.
He prays and watches both mother and baby—stunned.

This baby arrived amid a herd of horses,
horses of different colors.

White horses ride in on the breath of the wind.
White horses from the west
where plants of golden chamisa shimmer in the moonlight.

She arrived amid a herd of horses.
Yellow horses enter from the east
bringing the scent of prairie grasses from the small hills outside.

She arrived amid a herd of horses.

Blue horses rush in, snorting from the desert in the south.
It is possible to see across the entire valley to Niist'áá from Tó.
Bah, from here your grandmothers went to war long ago.

She arrived amid a herd of horses.

Black horses came from the north.
They are the lush summers of Montana and still white winters of Idaho.

Chamisa, Chamisa Bah. It is all this that you are.
You will grow: laughing, crying,
and we will celebrate each change you live.

You will grow strong like the horses of your past.
You will grow strong like the horses of your birth.

—Luci Tapahonso (Navajo)

Spokane woman on horseback with infant in baby carrier, 1899. Colville Reservation, Washington. P4178

Boy in traditional dress, on horseback, travois attached. P14191

This postcard is clearly a posed shot—women didn't wear feathers until later, and the boy is too young to have earned a war bonnet.

Postcard of a Sioux woman riding a horse with travois. P16728

Despite its somewhat patronizing caption, "This Indian hasn't any Ford but she gets there just the same," this postcard shows a more authentic shot of a travois in use.

This Indian hasn't any Ford but she gets there just the same.

Chaticksi (Pawnee) child on horseback.
P14190

Absaroke (Crow) girls, circa 1910.
Montana. Photograph by Fred R. Meyer.
N21901

Not seen often in photos, lance cases
such as the one pictured here typically
were used not to carry lances, but swords.